Puppies · The Sounds of Music · Seashells · Candlelight · Saying "I Love You" ·
Saying "I'm Sorry" · Flowers · Motherhood · A Good Book · Kindness · Afternoon Naps ·
Family · Thunderstorms · Sad Movies · Friends · Gratitude · Quiet Time ·
Independence · Imagination · Contentment · Milestones · Hugs · Sunrise · A Child's Art ·
The Smell of a New Baby · Romance · Holidays · Trust · Holding Hands ·
Charity · Summer Nights · Old Dogs · Family Dinners · A Good Cup of Coffee · Curiosity ·
A Sense of Wonder · Hope · Companionship · Home · Butterflies · Courage · You ·
Wisdom · Warm Spring Days · Memories · Honest Work · Faith · Bubble Baths · Passion ·
Puppies · The Sounds of Music · Seashells · Candlelight · Saying "I Love You" ·
Saying "I'm Sorry" · Flowers · Motherhood · A Good Book · Kindness · Afternoon Naps ·
Holidays · Thunderstorms · Sad Movies · Family · Gratitude · Quiet Time ·
Independence · Imagination · Contentment · Milestones · Hugs · Sunrise · A Child's Art ·
The Smell of a New Baby · Romance · Holidays · Trust · Sympathy · Flowers ·
Charity · Summer Nights · Old Dogs · Family Din   ee · Curiosity ·
Home · Butterflies · Coura   Memories ·
Honest Work · Faith · Bubble Bath   t · Charity ·
Flowers · Motherhood · A Good Boo   ss · Afternoon Naps · Friends ·
Thunderstorms · Sad Movies · Charity · Family · Gratitude · Quiet Time · Independence ·
Imagination · Milestones · Hugs · Sunrise · A Child's Art · Wisdom · Romance ·

Merry Christmas 2010

A gift for:

Peg

With Love.

From:

Becky - Larry

50
Things THAT REALLY
Matter

GIFT BOOKS
from Hallmark

BC

ODALE

This edition published in 2003 under license from Rodale Books exclusively for Hallmark Cards, Inc.

Printed and bound in China.

Cover Design by Hallmark Cards, Inc.

Interior Design by Uttley/DouPonce DesignWorks

16   18   20   19   17   15

www.hallmark.com

Contents

Introduction
Defining What Really Matters

ig homes. Luxury cars. Diamond bracelets. Digital TVs. Exotic vacations. Extravagant trips to the spa.

These days, we're surrounded by such symbols of wealth. And if we aren't among the lucky few to enjoy these prizes, we feel left out, stressed, perhaps even unworthy or depressed.

Why?

These aren't the things that really matter in life. Not by a long shot.

What matters most are the simple pleasures so abundant that we all can enjoy them; the plain values that define us as good people; the emotional connections with friends and family that fill our souls with a sense of purpose.

This book celebrates 50 of the simple things that really do matter in life. Within these pages are first-person stories about the value of conversing over a good cup of coffee, the importance of hugs, the courage in living a simple life, the wisdom in a street musician's words, the peace and relaxation in watching a candle flame.

May these stories encourage you, enlighten you, and enrich your soul. But most of all, may they inspire you to see the real value in life.

After all, happiness doesn't lie in the objects we gather around us. It lies within us. To find it, all we need do is open our eyes.

Wisdom

fter college and before I figured out what I wanted to do with my life, I bartended for 2 years in Boulder, Colorado. To pass the slow winter days, I befriended the elderly saxophonist who played outside the restaurant.

Eugene "Lucky" Hudson had lived each of his 75 years with a passion for experience that took him all over the country, playing juke joints and living out of suitcases. Every afternoon, I'd wipe the bar, and he'd listen to my stories—quibbles with coworkers, laments about holiday demands, wounds left over from spats with friends. Regardless of how silly or insipid that day's complaints were, Lucky would listen with his whole body, nodding and humming and closing his eyes, "tsk"ing and laughing with his whole belly. At the end of my rants, he'd wipe his beer mustache with the back of his hand, fix me with his huge brown eyes, and say, "Well, let me tell you something about people. . . ." and off he'd launch into a story.

At the time, I'd wonder what an anecdote about working a farm in Alabama or sporting around the jazz clubs of San Francisco had to do with my problems. I saw only the specific details of his situations, the distinct personalities he described. Now, with the benefit of a few experiences of my own, I see those details as markers, giving tangible form to the real messages behind his words.

When I remember those words, I no longer hear about the rough drought in back in 1939 or the gleam of a fin-tailed Cadillac. I hear his low, smooth voice saying, "Your momma just needs to be loved—don't question it, just do it" or "Forgiveness is our chance to create divinity—granting it only begets more."

What swim back to me with complete and ruthless clarity are the lessons he tossed around as effortlessly as seeds from a farmer's hand. Those seeds took root, and I'm only now hearing his wisdom as clearly as he heard my woes.

BY MARISKA VAN AALST

His devotion to our springtime ritual
showed his **devotion to me—**
not only to my love of baseball
but also to my life.

Warm Spring Days

hen I was young, it wasn't love that filled my thoughts in the spring. It was baseball.

I loved everything about the game—the crack of a bat, the thrill of chasing a ground ball across short green grass, even watching the games on our old black-and-white TV. Yet looking back now, no ceremony was quite as important to me as the annual ritual of playing catch with my dad.

Dad was never much of a baseball fan, but as green leaves began to sprout on barren branches and warmth returned to the air, he would grab his old mitt and head out to the yard with me just the same. There was something therapeutic about playing catch with him. The hum of the ball as it sailed through the air. The friendly pop as it hit the leather netting. We may have been 50 feet apart, but the flight of that ball connected us, forming as strong a bond as any father-son talk ever could have.

I was never the star of my Little League team, yet Dad never cared about that. Every year, he would be out there, waiting to field any errant throw I sent his way.

As I grew older, I realized that our game was a reflection of our relationship—that even if a problem didn't involve a glove and a ball, Dad would always be there to handle anything I threw in his direction. His devotion to our springtime ritual showed his devotion to me—not only to my love of baseball but also to my life.

I've often heard it said that "the devil is in the details." Now I realize that in my relationship with my father, love was in the details.

BY WYATT MYERS

THREE

Memories

e recently moved to a small town dotted with cemeteries dating back to well before the Civil War. Wandering through them on early-morning and late-evening walks with my dog, I often stop to read the carefully carved, worn stones. The dates—from birth to death—reveal so much. There are parents and grandparents. There are soldiers and their widows. And children—infants even. I like to say their names aloud, in some small way confirming that these people really did exist—that even though they left this world long ago, they're still a precious part of some family's memories.

My grandma died almost 35 years ago, and I have not been back to her grave since we buried her. Yet my memories of her are clear. I still have split-seconds of wanting to call her—maybe to tell her about the new dress I just bought or the good-looking guy I saw at the grocery store. She always wanted to know the latest piece of news, no matter how trivial. My mother says that those momentary thoughts keep Grandma in my heart.

Maybe. But just as important to me now is the thought that perhaps another woman is walking with her dog through the cemetery where Grandma is buried. If so, I hope she will brush off the headstone to read the dates and to say my grandmother's name aloud, doing her part to keep Grandma's memory alive.

BY ELLEN MAZO

I like to say their names aloud, **confirming** that these people are still a **precious part** of some family's memory.

Honest Work

 hen my husband, Matt, was about 10 years old, his grandfather started taking him to the family cherry tree orchards on Saturday afternoons. Matt would work alongside the farmhands, whistling as he went, to let his grandfather know he wasn't eating any of the cherries intended for the bushel. A full day's work netted Matt 50 cents. If his grandfather bought him a hot dog and a soda, they called it even.

As a teenager, his dad would call up from the breakfast table, "Two minutes!" Matt knew better than to challenge—he was dressed, fed, and out raking leaves or tilling soil before the sun had risen over the ridge.

I was horrified by these stories during our first years together. I mourned for his lost childhood, thinking gratefully of my Saturday mornings in front of cartoons, slurping cereal. After we were married, though, I noticed how quickly he'd be done with his chores while I was still cursing over the dishes. His focus was intense but cheerful. He got the job done well and quickly because he put himself completely into the task—because he'd learned to enjoy honest work.

No matter if he's cleaning the gutters or finishing a report, Matt embraces each project as an opportunity for expression. His lovingly stirred spaghetti sauce says, "I feed and nourish our family." His well-weeded garden says, "I savor my connection to the earth." Through example after example, he demonstrates the key to happiness in whatever we do. Matt's lesson: All work—on the field, in the factory, or on the computer—can be honest and fulfilling, if we approach it from a place of devotion.

As Matt has shown me, honest work is our contribution to the community and to the world, the outward

All work—on the field, in the factory, or on the computer— can be honest and fulfilling, if we approach it from a place of devotion.

manifestation of our soul's purpose. Just as the trees keep the air clean, give us shade, and shower us with fruits and nuts, so too are we each charged with our task, creating the future, one brick—or compost pile or database or cherry pie—at a time.

BY MARISKA VAN AALST

Faith

here's an old story about Jeb and the flood that tells us something important about faith. Old Jeb was trapped on his roof as the flood-waters were rising around his house. As he sat there, a neighbor passed by in his rowboat, offering to take him to higher ground.

"Don't worry about me," said Jeb. "I have faith: The Lord will protect me."

A while later, the floodwaters still rising, a rescue squad arrived in a powerboat and ordered Jeb to evacuate. "No need," Jeb insisted. "My faith is strong. I'll be fine."

A few hours later, when the waters reached the eaves, a

National Guard helicopter hovered overhead and lowered a line. But Jeb wouldn't grab hold. "The Lord will provide," he said.

Not too long after, Jeb's house went under, and Jeb with it. When he arrived at the pearly gates, he was none too pleased.

"Lord, I had such faith in you!" Jeb cried. "How could you have abandoned me?"

"Abandon you?" replied the Lord. "What are you talking about? I sent you a rowboat, a powerboat, and a helicopter!"

Like many of us, Jeb had great faith, but it was a faith built only upon miracles that come with flashes of light and trumpet blasts. In truth, God often responds to our faith in humbler ways. It might be a kind driver who lets us merge when we're stressed from sitting in heavy traffic. Or it could be a newspaper article that describes a support group we desperately need. Or perhaps it comes in a song on the radio that brings us a cherished, fortifying memory.

Each day, angels visit the doorsteps of the faithful, leaving gifts that quietly offer God's grace, comfort, and protection. All we have to do is recognize them and pick them up.

BY DOUG HILL

I lay back and ponder words like "relaxation," "peace," "tranquillity," "alone," and even "ahh."

Bubble Baths

 here's something magical about a bath. It can become a refuge from the outside world in a way that a shower simply can't. Add bubbles to the mix, and I'm instantly transported into another world.

There needs to be mountains of bubbles for it to be a *real* bubble bath, whether those bubbles are created from regular dishwashing soap or some fancy floral-scented concoction from a specialty shop. With the bathroom door closed, the shower curtain drawn to keep out the drafts, and a candle lit somewhere nearby, I'm in my own secluded little world. I run the water as hot as I can stand it—nearly blanching myself in the process. I sink in and spend the first few minutes heating up, releasing tension, and cherishing the bubbly bliss.

Then I lay back and ponder words like "relaxation," "peace," "tranquillity," "alone," and even "ahh." I inhale them along with the tub's steam, then exhale any negative feelings. As the heat evaporates into the steamy bathroom air, taking along my muscle aches, I send my heartaches with it. I swish my hands under the water, creating gentle currents of soothing calm. With my eyes closed, I tune in to the sounds of the suds snapping. Then I take a deep breath and submerge, drowning out any other cares I may have.

As the flame of the candle flickers outside the tub, I know it is my spirit reviving and dancing, eagerly awaiting my body to resurface and join life again.

BY JENNIFER S. KUSHNIER

Passion

My father wore suits and ties for 30 years. But his hands were, and are, those of an artist. They transform marble into sculpture, coax herbs and vegetables from the earth, and cook meals that would bring tears to your eyes. Everything he touches turns to art.

Not everyone can have talented hands like his. But we each harbor the same ability to be passionate about our lives.

All we have to do is search our hearts for our special passion.

Passion satisfies a vital spiritual need: the need for connection. It's the feeling we get when we're in tune with something larger than ourselves. Passion makes us feel alive, makes us certain that we walk this planet for some purpose.

Opportunities to experience passion are everywhere. Sometimes they're quiet, like growing prizewinning tomatoes or creating beauty and delight with a sewing needle, gardening spade, or mixing bowl. Sometimes they speak ringingly and draw us to our faith, a social cause, or civic involvement.

Like a battery powers a car, passion powers our souls. Without it, our hearts go hungry.

My father doesn't talk about passion. His hands do. Each chisel-cut knuckle and earth-grimed nail says: To find your passion, open your heart and let the world flood in.

BY JULIA VANTINE

Puppies

y husband, Matt, wanted to get a dog for years, but I always resisted. "We'll be chained down," I said. "Think of the dog hair!" I whined. Then a neighbor put up a sign advertising her litter of yellow labs. I relented, baby Lulu came home with us, and she started teaching me lessons about life—one lick at a time.

Within 24 hours of her arrival, I was reduced to a human dust mop, shimmying around the floor, gripping plastic toys and squeaking, "Oh, such a sweet little girl! Give Mommy a kiss!" (Lulu Lesson #1: When you're really enjoying play, you don't care how foolish you look.)

Soon, Matt and I both were hooked. We'd fret over her whining. We would buy books on how to socialize her. We fed her by hand. Against all good judgment and advice, we'd let her sleep with us. She repaid us—with poops on the carpet. (Lulu Lesson #2: Parenting can make you more neurotic than you've ever dreamed possible.)

Before Lulu arrived, I'd sleep until 8:30 A.M. one day; the next, I'd be up at dawn. Now Lulu will be standing on my chest by the time the sun crests the horizon, demanding to get out the door within the next 15 minutes. (Lulu Lesson #3: Ritual is the glue that holds love together.)

Although I used to stay at work late, I now can't wait to get home at night. When I arrive, Lulu will be standing on a chair, peeking out the window. And the moment I cross the threshold, I'll be rewarded with what feels like the kind of welcome normally reserved for pro athletes and legendary rock stars. A few licks, and I can forget the petty details of the day. (Lulu Lesson #4: Unconditional love is a renewable resource.)

We've learned to read her body signals: the cocked

head of curiosity; the ears pressed back with excitement and adoration; the sigh that comes from deep within a warm, rubbed belly. Even one of her looks almost knocks me off my feet: "You're a dog," I'll think. "But what great conversations we've been having!" (Lulu Lesson #5: True communication is only possible when we don't rely upon language.)

BY MARISKA VAN AALST

As my experience showed, music can heal the soul. It has the power to create inner peace and harmony.

NINE

The Sounds of Music

riedrich Nietzsche once said that "without music, life would be a mistake." I found the truth in those words several years ago, at a time when I had no music in my life.

I felt like something was terribly wrong, like I was losing my mind, but I couldn't figure out the problem. One cold November night, I tried to sort things out by running to the top of the highest mountain near my house. When I reached the top, sharp gusts of wind nipped at my ears. I stood there, wondering what to do next, when I swear I heard the wind shouting at me: "Listen! Listen!"

Astonished and bewildered, I cried out, "Listen to what?"

But there was only silence.

I listened to that cold silence for nearly an hour.

Finally, I realized the silence itself was the answer. It was pointing out the void that music once had filled. When I was younger, I had always played music: piano at home; baritone horn in grade school; drums in high school. But in the 2 years before my visit to the mountaintop, I hadn't even listened to the radio.

I climbed down the mountain and joined a local musical group the very next week. One month later, my unhappiness was gone—my spirits lifted by the rhythm and melody of live music. To this day, music cures whatever ails me.

As my experience showed, music can heal the soul. It has the power to create inner peace and harmony. Any type of recorded or live music can have this soothing, comforting effect: the gentle strum of an acoustic guitar; the deep groove of a jazz trio. These and other sounds are music to my ears. And they can be to yours, too. All you have to do is listen.

BY DAVID JOACHIM

Seashells

or me, seashells are the best proof that there's a creator. Buried in the dark, sandy seafloor or living hundreds—even thousands—of feet below the ocean's surface, these fragile, uniquely beautiful "houses" go unseen.

While their occupants are alive, the intricate shapes and patterns of the seashells often are concealed beneath a fleshy covering, their beauty serving no apparent purpose. Shells could be plain and serviceable and still fulfill their protective role. But instead, they feature exquisite forms and colors.

I like to think the beauty is there to remind us of the

The beauty is there
to remind us of the
one who created
the diverse beauty of our
world for His own delight.

one who created the diverse beauty of our world for His own delight.

Each time I hold a shell, I, too, feel that delight and am reminded that sometimes, like shells, our true beauty is only apparent after we've passed from our Earthly life.

BY ELLEN PHILLIPS

E L E V E N

Candlelight

he next time you light a candle to brighten a room, take a few minutes to gaze into its flame. As it dances and flickers, put yourself inside that flame.

It has a life and a spirit of its own, just as we all do. Like the flame, we each expel a warmth. The hottest part of a candle's flame is the part nearest the wick, where the light glows blue. Like that flame, we too may have a blueness inside us. But remember, we have a similar radiance, with the capacity to warm our surroundings and brighten any room we enter.

BY JENNIFER S. KUSHNIER

Remember, we have a similar
radiance about us, with
**the capacity to
warm** our surroundings
and **brighten any room**
we enter.

We will never forget the man who taught us that **the best way to say** "I love you" often has little to do with the words.

Saying "I Love You"

hen I was in college, a man named Henry worked as a custodian in our student union building. White-haired, with a Pennsylvania Dutch accent, Henry could usually be seen in a baseball cap, a T-shirt, and a pair of jeans with a big silver belt buckle.

He was the custodian, and he was the most respected and most well-known person in the building. Everyone loved Henry, and it was because of all the subtle ways he expressed his love for everyone around him. Henry didn't have to say, "I love you." He lived his love.

Henry was always excited when he met someone new, and he wanted to know everything about them. He felt it was important to do things for people he valued. And Henry seemed to value everyone he met. He brought in articles or cartoons for certain people, went out of his way to introduce people to each other, kept track of dozens of names and birthdays in his wallet so he could send cards, and helped students keep in touch with graduates who had written him. He even discretely assisted students who didn't have enough money to buy their books.

Henry taught me—and many others he befriended—how to live life to the fullest. Not by skydiving or exploring some exotic country, but by appreciating where you are in life and valuing those around you.

The funny thing is that despite all he did and taught us, Henry truly believed that he was the lucky one—that he was the one who was gaining so much by getting to know us. But all of us who remember Henry know that we were the ones who were truly blessed.

We will never forget the man who taught us that the best way to say "I love you" often has little to do with the words.

BY SANDY HEIERBACHER

THIRTEEN

Saying "I'm Sorry"

ne day, when I was in college, a shifty-looking character approached me in the student union with a leather jacket he wanted to sell. It was a beauty: buttery smooth cowhide, with artfully stitched seams and long leather fringes. Buffalo Bill Cody would have worn it proudly.

I can't remember what the price was, but it was obviously too little for such a jacket. Even as I forked over the money, I knew something wasn't right. Sure enough, a couple days later, the jacket's real owner, a student about my age, approached me as I was on my way to class.

"That's my jacket," he said, "and I want it back."

"No way," I answered. "I paid for it, and I have no idea if it's yours. It's mine."

He didn't challenge me, and I left, but the uneasiness I had about my new possession now had a visible face. A few days later, riding my bike across campus, I saw the real owner standing on the sidewalk. I rode over, took the jacket off, handed it to him, said I was sorry, and rode off without another word. More than the weight of the jacket had been lifted from my shoulders.

We're all human, which means that sometimes we do things we shouldn't do or say things we shouldn't say. Sometimes we realize too late that our actions have been hurtful to somebody else. When these hard times occur, the best response—the only response, really—is, "I'm sorry."

Owning up, promptly and forthrightly, helps the other person begin to heal. But just as important, it cleanses our own soul and sets us free.

That is a small price to pay for a clear conscience.

BY DOUG HILL

Owning up, promptly and forthrightly, helps the other person begin to heal. But just as important, it cleanses our own soul and sets us free.

Flowers

eople often send flowers to cheer up someone after an accident or a loss in the family. My father proved there's an even better use.

A few years ago, he was diagnosed with a brain tumor. It was a stressful, scary, emotional roller-coaster time for everyone in my family.

The tumor was the size of a golf ball and located close to his ear. The doctors said that the surgery would be very complicated and was likely to cost my father the hearing in one ear and paralyze half his face. But it was absolutely necessary.

So they wheeled him into the operating room and worked on him for 12½ hours. Thankfully, my dad came through the operation okay, and the tumor was benign. Still, he spent many weeks in the hospital, recovering from the surgery and at one point fighting meningitis. After that came long months of recovery.

Through it all, my mom never left his side. She took care of him, loved him, made him comfortable, and sat by him through his entire recovery time. She gave all of herself to him.

On the 1-year anniversary of my dad's surgery, he acknowledged how important she had been to him. He sent my mom a beautiful flower arrangement and included a card with this message: "I know this day last year was a lot longer for you than it was for me. Thank you for being there then, now—and always."

For once the roles reversed, and it wasn't the person who was sick who got the flowers. It was the person who loved unconditionally and with all of her heart.

As Dad showed, it's important to celebrate the people who hold your hand and never let go. They're the true heroes.

BY LEANNE COPPOLA

Finally **comprehending** that I am the unquestionable center of my daughter's universe let me experience **motherhood** at its truest.

FIFTEEN

Motherhood

ike many first-time moms, I've often felt unmotherlike—as if I'm somehow less than qualified to be in charge of a human life. I had expected to bond instantly with my newborn daughter and through that bond, mother her instinctively. Yet just after Willa's birth, when I searched her eyes for that connection, I saw nothing but my reflection. The instincts I had anticipated were hidden somewhere deep within me.

A few storybook moments during Willa's early babyhood inspired me to say, "Yes, this is it. I'm her mother." Times like when I heard her first laugh, when I soothed her sobbing, when I finally got her to sleep through the night. Unfortunately, the good ones were outnumbered by other, less-than-perfect instances—times I thought, "I'm not fit to be anyone's mom." Like when I carried a 4-month-old Willa out of the nursery on my shoulders, remembering too late that the top of the doorjamb hung lower than the ceiling. Willa's head hit it with a loud thud, and she unleashed one of those wails that starts out silent, then breaks your heart with its intertwined pain and panic.

Add to this Willa's long running "daddy phase," when only my husband seemed good enough for her, and I have to say I struggled emotionally during our first year-and-a-half as mother and daughter.

Then came the moment I felt a true bond for the first time, and with it that elusive mother instinct. We sat together on an antique train at a railway museum one early September day after Willa had turned 19 months old. She cemented into my lap as the locomotive began to chug along the tracks and stared wide-eyed at the passing scenery. Through her stillness, I could sense her fear and excitement as she absorbed the brand-new experience. Her 25-pound body felt more like 100. To me, that heaviness expressed her absolute expectation that my lap would protect her as we embarked on this adventure. All of her eggs rested in my basket, as it were. It moved me to the core.

Of course, there's no single experience that defines universal motherhood. For me, finally comprehending that I am the unquestionable center of my daughter's universe let me experience motherhood at its truest. I don't need much more than that.

BY LEAH FLICKINGER

Sixteen

A Good Book

e swim in words all day long—stock quotes, headlines that scream, to-do lists, insurance forms, the occasional fashion magazine or dime-store romance. Yet for all their power to occupy or distract us, these types of writing will never compare to a good book.

A really good book doesn't just entertain; it leaves you fundamentally different. It's both a mirror and a magnifying glass—a woven compilation of seemingly small details that has the power to show you your truest self. When you read a good book, you see that everyone's problems are the same, but they're just a jumping-off point—that there are as many ways to live as there are grains of salt in the sea.

How do you know when you've found a good book? Time melts as you read it. Unsuspecting, you crack the spine and find yourself whisked to a place that sings to every cell in your body. Soon you're befriending characters that become soul mates, following a story that seems truer than reality.

Indeed, in the middle of a good book, you become so wrapped up in the story that you forget about the language, the way an exquisite painting renders color transparent. No one word, or hue, stands out as the most beautiful—they are all elemental, irreplaceable, in one complete, perfectly balanced whole.

Then, as you near the end of the book, you start metering out the pages in small doses because you don't want to leave the special world you've entered.

Most of all, a good book inspires you. As the words flow in and out of you, they change your attitude and open you up to new experiences. Read long enough, and a good book can make you want to be a better person, live a better life, talk to strangers, jet off to Paris, pick up a pen to write your own stories.

Next time a good book finds you, take a moment to give thanks for how one object, no bigger than the span of two palms, can contain so much of the world, teach you so much of what it means to be human, and make you feel so alive.

BY MARISKA VAN AALST

Kindness

n college, I was among a group of student activists who constructed a makeshift shanty-town, where we planned to sleep to raise awareness of homelessness. On the night of the event, a group of men living at a nearby emergency shelter found out and asked if they could join us.

A few students were afraid of getting closer than we'd planned to witnesses of the harsh issue we were tackling. But our visitors turned out to be kind and gentle souls who kept us up all night telling their stories.

We learned how three of them had come from Mexico, intending to make money to send to their families. When they found no work, they had become stranded. One guest was born in an orphanage and said being homeless was simply the only way of life he knew. My favorite, Earl, was having trouble getting back on his feet after spending time in prison for a minor crime. Nobody thought enough of him to give him a secure place to live, but, as he showed us, he was brilliant enough to design plans for an entire underground city.

The next morning, we left our new friends and made our way to the school cafeteria. The cafeteria staff served us mounds of waffles and omelets, which they said were "on them."

We knew there had to be a powerful force at work to make things turn out so well: The college administration could have panicked and tried to stop us when we revealed our plans to sleep in cardboard boxes. The homeless men could have easily been cynical and dismissed us students as pampered do-gooders. We students could have rejected our homeless visitors, fearing the stereotypes that were simply not true.

Instead, we all shared a cup of true kindness—and were better for it.

This experience taught me that when it comes to kindness, there is very little difference between who is giving it and who is receiving it. And we all have access to the exchange of warmth and nourishment kindness brings our souls. We just need to trust enough to open our hearts. The rest will take care of itself.

BY MARY S. KITTEL

Falling asleep isn't the point.
It's the act of curling up
with a mom-made afghan,
and letting myself
think or dream
of anything I want.

EIGHTEEN

Afternoon Naps

ike most children, I dreaded taking afternoon naps when I was young. I imagined all kinds of thrilling fun that adults had while I slumbered away. I couldn't wait until I turned 5, that magical year when my mother freed me and all the kids she's ever taken care of from our daily drudgery.

Then, as a college student, my attitude turned an about-face. I came to cherish naptime, whether it was mid-morning, after lunch, or early evening—and sometimes all three. When I began working after college, the one thing I sorely missed was that freedom to lie down and steal a half-hour snooze whenever I wanted. Still today, many moons later, I miss that freedom and love when I can indulge in the bliss of a wink or two.

On the days I am not working, I always set aside time to rest. Whether I actually fall asleep isn't the point. It's the act of lying down, curling up with a mom-made afghan, closing my eyes, and letting myself think or dream of anything I want. I don't have to do any figuring or complex thinking. I can listen to music, turn on a daytime talk show, or count the sparkles in my ceiling if I want to. I can even imagine the thrilling fun other adults are having as I lie there at peace with myself.

That afternoon nap is the one time of my day when I can be private and keep to myself—and remind myself what good company I am.

BY JENNIFER S. KUSHNIER

NINETEEN

Friends

nce in a while, you make friends who have the power to restore your faith in humanity. Once in the greatest of whiles, you make friends who can restore your faith in yourself.

I moved into a small town right before the weather changed one year, and it looked like I was in for a cold, lonely winter—away from my friends and my life in the city. Then a colleague from work casually invited me to dinner and a movie with her "chick flick" group. Thirsty for female companionship, I jumped at the chance.

I imagined there would be light chatter about celebrities—the way my old friends and I had passed time. But as we sat at the dinner table, one woman said, "Time for check-in!" Each woman then took a turn relating, with deep-felt emotion, what was going on in her life while the other six gave their full attention.

I was uncomfortable. This sharing among friends was more intimate than anything I'd experienced before. The waiter came to the table before it was time for my check-in, and I was secretly relieved.

The next time, and the next, and the next, I kept my mouth closed. When pressed, I would blurt out something simple: "I'm happy it's the weekend!" or "I'll be seeing my family for the holidays." I couldn't bring myself to tell all. Yet the 12 eyes portrayed no sense of disappointment, just the same focused attention they devoted to each other.

One night, I'd just come from an encounter at work that left me devastated, and my check-in came. Before I could stop myself, I told them of my worst fears—that I might not cut it and I'd be fired. I was searching to make sense of everything, but I was so torn and confused. Then as I talked, my fears, buried and knotted deep in my belly, broke up and lightened and started to float. I saw myself reflected back in their eyes: a just, honest soul. Someone who had a lot to be proud of. Someone worthy of respect and understanding. Someone worthy of friendship.

Since that day, I crave the check-ins like a cloudless blue sky in a dull gray winter. As I've learned, the power of loving friends who are willing to devote their entire attention to you is as healing as any force on Earth.

BY MARISKA VAN AALST

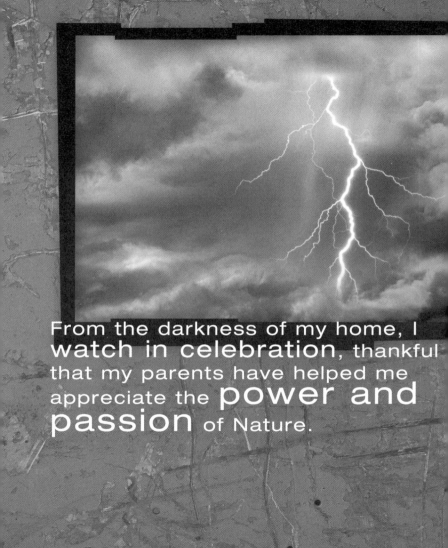

From the darkness of my home, I watch in celebration, thankful that my parents have helped me appreciate the power and passion of Nature.

Thunderstorms

he crack and fury of a thunderstorm might strike fear in some people, but I learned early on to appreciate Mother Nature's light-and-sound show. When I was young, each time a storm approached, my parents would usher my sister and me out onto the front porch. There, in safety, we would watch the world change.

Dark clouds would muffle the sunlight, and the sky, after a low rumble, would open up and give our metal swing set a shower. Rain seeping into the grass released a smell of dirt into the air. Sooner or later, a swoosh of rubber through water would announce the approach of a car. We'd watch it splash by, its windshield wipers tossing water aside.

My parents would play up the drama, telling us that the rumbles and cracks we heard were the sounds of angels bowling overhead. Our hearts racing, my sister and I would count the seconds between the bright flash of lightning and the loud crash of thunder to see how close the angels were. Finally, with disappointment, we'd listen as the thunder got weaker and weaker until the storm passed, and the sun peaked through the clouds again.

To my parents, thunderstorms weren't a danger, they were just a part of nature—to be experienced and enjoyed like any other. Through their attitudes, they taught us to feel that way too.

Even today, thunderstorms fascinate me. When others run for cover as a storm rolls overhead, I turn off the lights and put match to candles. Then from the darkness of my home, I watch in celebration, thankful that my parents have helped me appreciate the power and passion of Nature.

BY MARIE SUSZYNSKI

Sad Movies

 hen I was 16, I went to the movies with my 18-year-old stepbrother, Matt. He suggested the Disney movie *Beauty and the Beast*. I was pleased, but a little taken aback (I had prepared myself for car chases and explosions).

I loved the movie; it was romantic, touching, and colorful. But I kept thinking, "Matt must be bored to tears over there." Then came the scene where Belle and the Beast dance. I got completely caught up in it. They danced so beautifully together, and the Beast was surprisingly graceful despite his beastliness—what a shame he had to be trapped in that ferocious form.

I heard sniffles, and I figured it was some romantic girl like me. But the sniffles were a little too close. I looked over, and it was Matt who was crying—star football player and prom king. And they weren't tears of boredom—the movie was really getting to him. He noticed my stare. "It's sad," he said, unashamed.

It *was* sad. Inspired by Matt, I, too, let loose and cried alongside him. In that shared moment, the two of us really connected for the first time.

Sad movies can provide special moments like that for all of us. They can help us connect emotionally with the rest of the audience in a way we never would outside those four walls. It's comforting, too, to know that when a scene turns saddest, everyone around—from strangers to teenage stepbrothers—may feel like crying, too.

BY ELIZABETH SHIMER

Family

he bulletin board in my office is almost as large as a mural and very much my master-piece—a photographic potpourri of so many children in my life, yet none of them mine. Each time I glance up, I understand how family can be extended, and precious, without being biological.

Several pictures are of my handsome nephews, Ben and Sam, now grown. There's Daniel and Michael, also adult children who still call me Auntie. Two photos are of David and Emily. Their parents, both sets of their grandparents, and I traveled with them to Israel to celebrate their coming of religious age in a moving ceremony.

Then there's Katie, defiantly bald after braving chemotherapy to conquer her cancer. And Molly and Lia, sisters celebrating their special friendship. Impish Lily is swathed in a silk scarf I found in Jerusalem's Old City.

The latest is Tong Yan, hugging a soft toy rabbit. Friends Peg and Bill traveled halfway around the world to adopt this beautiful toddler, found abandoned in a railroad station in China. In her photo, she is staring at me shyly, her dark eyes glistening with the same anticipation we all felt during the days before her new parents were to meet her for the first time.

Peg and Bill had waited months for a child, as their plans became entangled in endless legal papers. After they headed off to China, I waited, too, for a message about this newest family member. Finally, the recognizable "You've Got Mail" tone sounded from the computer, and Bill's e-mail announcement of their frenzied journey appeared: "Arrived in Hong Kong after 24 hours, 3 bad movies, 2.5 mediocre meals, 1 book each and numerous naps," Bill wrote. "Slept. Whirlwind tour of city. Four-hour bus ride to

Guanzhou Airport. One hour, 15-minute flight to Hefei. Thirty-minute bus ride to hotel. Meeting (15 families). Dinner. Slept. Elaborate breakfast buffet."

Then, finally, Peg and Bill met Tong Yan face-to-face. Bill summed up their feelings in three words: "Gift from God."

Tong Yan is now part of my bulletin board family too, a precious member to be cherished like the rest. Another "gift from God."

BY ELLEN MAZO

I am grateful, too,
for the time I spent with her,
the laughter we shared, and the
wonderful
memories I have.

TWENTY-THREE

Gratitude

y mother definitely had her share of troubles raising me and my four sisters. But she was always there for us, never turning her back at times when it must have been difficult. Through the years, she became as much my friend as my mother.

We spent a lot of time together, going to bingo every weekend and taking trips, including a spur-of-the-moment girls' weekend. There was always laughter, good times, and good memories.

One morning, when Mom was just 58, I received a phone call telling me that she had collapsed. She had survived a heart attack 7 months before. This time, the doctor said, she had a brain aneurysm. There was heavy bleeding, evident damage to her left side, and surgery was necessary.

After hours of surgery, she was unconscious, but she recognized our presence and squeezed our hands when we asked her to. For hours we talked to her, encouraging her to fight as she deteriorated. Soon there were complications, and she was not responding. Our words changed.

Mom always made clear that she would not want to live either on life support or if she could not care for herself. We watched her lying there, helpless. Finally we said, "Mom, please fight if you can; we need you here with us. But if you are tired, and you want us to let you go and you don't want to fight anymore, don't worry about anything; it will be fine. Do what you need to do." Soon she was no longer breathing on her own, and it became apparent that it wasn't my mother lying in that bed, but instead a body functioning on machines. We knew what had to be done, and the life support was disconnected. On my youngest sister's birthday, Mom officially passed away.

Afterward, we had to go home and explain to her 13 grandchildren that Gram had died; she wouldn't be coming home. As anyone who has children knows, their pain is harder to handle than your own. Talking to them was one of the hardest things I've ever had to do.

I thank God that my mother was adamant about her beliefs and wishes, making our decision at the hospital as easy as such a thing could ever be. I am grateful, too, for the time I spent with her, the laughter we shared, and the wonderful memories I have. Two years have passed, and these memories still bring laughter to my heart and tears to my eyes.

BY PAT MAST

TWENTY-FOUR

Quiet Time

 rode next to my mother in the family car for 16 years. When my legs were still swinging free from my car seat, and for a few years after I graduated to just a seat belt, we sang nursery rhymes together. Then we moved on to singing along with a tape or the radio—sometimes top 10 (my choice at that age), and sometimes The Beatles or Rolling Stones (her choice). But there were always those occasional moments when she would turn the music off without warning and say, "I just want quiet."

Those words used to make me so frustrated—"but I was just getting into the song!" I would protest. Sometimes she'd give in and turn it on again, and sometimes she was steadfast. She just wanted quiet.

Today, I understand. Quiet is precious. Sometimes quiet clears the way for sounds we rarely stop to appreciate, like the trickling of a stream, a ticking clock, or even just the hum of the car motor. At other times, quiet completely takes over, like during a snowstorm—birds hop on the snow, squirrels run around, but nothing makes a sound. It's just quiet.

The other day, I was riding in the car with my mom. She had the radio on, and I reached over and turned it off. I didn't have to explain myself—she knew why I did it. In a world full of honking horns, blaring music, echoing restaurants, and TV commercials so loud they make the dog run and hide, sometimes I, too, just want quiet.

BY ELIZABETH SHIMER

Sometimes, leaving a world dense with memories is necessary for the soul to continue to prosper.

Independence

 grew up in a house the color of pink pearls. To negate the silly color when describing it to visiting friends, I always made sure to emphasize the shutters, which were a respectable black.

Recently, my mother spoke of selling our home, and even though its fanciful color had caused me years of embarrassment, I suddenly felt unnerved to be losing this link to my past. The thought of strangers preening in the unforgiving glare of my bathroom light was appalling. Surely, the blue-green carpet, worn from the drag of the piano bench, would be replaced with a coarse new one. The walls that captured the smells of Easter ham and Christmas pine would undoubtedly be smothered with paint. And what of the kitchen where my mother and I spoke of school and boyfriends over the sizzle of pork chops?

How could she abandon the web of memories we had spun over the decades? Perhaps for the same reason I left years ago: to honor a mushrooming independence.

Mom raised her daughters to be strong enough to fly away. After her children moved on and her husband died, she herself felt the need for flight.

Despite my newly discovered affection for that home, I have to respect her desire to move on—to test her own independence and all the excitement and challenges it will bring. So, I wish her steady winds, brilliant horizons, and seamless landings. And to the future occupants of the old homestead, I wish an appreciation for pink.

Independence, no matter when it comes, is fraught with emotions. The place we leave behind is embedded with priceless fingerprints. Sometimes, though, leaving a world dense with memories is necessary for the soul to continue to prosper.

BY SANDRA SALERA LLOYD

Imagination

hen I was very young, I thought the sky was blue because the Earth was suspended inside a blue ball that God bounced through the universe for His pleasure. I still believe that imagination is about seeing: First, about seeing what is, and then, about seeing what is possible.

I'm particularly drawn to the beauty of the natural world, and I use specific "sightings"—a red-tailed hawk soaring through the woods above the walking track at work or brilliant yellow maple leaves against the ever-green of ivy on a gray tree trunk under a clear fall sky—as incidents to spin into a poem or part of a novel, or translate into a vibrant quilt pattern or water-colored scene on an Easter egg.

But imagination for each of us is about more than physically seeing—it's also about "seeing" connections between seemingly unconnected things. We may pick up the colors of a favorite scene in the yarns of a sweater or scarf. (And the peaceful, repetitive nature of knitting is ideal for freeing our minds to imagine other things, too—like an attractive arrangement for next summer's garden or a new recipe for cookies.)

Ultimately, whatever way we use our imagination, we are telling a story. And the more unusual connections we see, the richer and more interesting our creations—our stories—will be.

Why do we see the sky as a blue vault, when a dog sees it as gray and a butterfly sees a faceted prism? Perhaps because we are wondrously made in a world whose glories shine like flames to light the fires of our imaginations. Or perhaps because we live at the center of a great blue ball.

BY ELLEN PHILLIPS

But imagination for each of us is about more than physically seeing—it's also about "seeing" connections between seemingly unconnected things.

Contentment really lies in finding a little happiness in whatever life throws your way.

Contentment

hile working as a Peace Corps volunteer in the Ukraine, I decided to take a trip to Budapest, Hungary. Traveling in that part of the world wasn't easy then—the old Soviet bureaucracy was still in place, and the mass transit system dated to a different age. In fact, just to buy a train ticket to Budapest, I was told I had to go to Stree, a small town 4 hours by train from the town in which I was living.

Undaunted, I left for Stree early one January morning. After a lengthy trip, I headed immediately to the ticket window. There, I asked the clerk for a ticket to Budapest and quickly learned that I had been misinformed. Tickets to Budapest weren't sold in Stree. The entire trip had been a waste. On top of that, I had to spend the entire day in this tiny, frozen town before I could catch the train back home.

By the time I boarded the return train, I was feeling hungry, exhausted, and angry that I had made such a long trip for nothing. But as I calmed down, I began to notice the many happy people around me. Most of them were village farmers—I could tell by their rough hands and clothes. Chances are, they had never met before and would never see each other again. Yet they were chatting pleasantly with each other, seemingly unperturbed by the cold weather, the problems of train travel, and any of the other things that had been occupying me. For the length of the journey, they were like old friends, happy to pass time together.

As I watched these people, it occurred to me that here was the perfect definition of contentment. Most of us think contentment means having everything you wish for. But as these farmers proved, contentment really lies in finding a little happiness in whatever life throws your way.

I sat back in a contentment of my own, realizing that the trip to Stree hadn't been a waste of time after all.

BY MARY S. MESAROS

We **owe it to ourselves** to recognize our milestones, to commemorate them, and to **use them as an opportunity** to reflect on and further our personal growth.

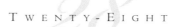

Milestones

his year, I celebrate my 11th year of sobriety. To a recovering alcoholic, each day that passes without "picking up" is a milestone.

But I have to admit, I'm proud . . . and grateful.

These 4,015 days (and counting) haven't always been easy. But they've been real. No lost days or nights. No hangovers. And few regrets, which had proliferated like dandelions in my drinking life.

So I celebrate this particular succession of days because each one has led me toward other milestones that have illuminated my life like so many little firecrackers.

Giving birth to my son.

Getting a divorce.

Making my first true female friend—and being a friend to other women.

Forging an emotional reconnection with my mom after years of mutual recrimination and misunderstandings.

This is just the short list.

My major milestone isn't an obvious one, like a high school graduation or a 50th wedding anniversary. But like fingerprints, milestones are unique. All of our lives have had their individual twists and turns. Milestones—in whatever form they take—allow us to measure how far we've come and to celebrate the journey.

We owe it to ourselves to recognize our milestones, to commemorate them, and to use them as an opportunity to reflect on and further our personal growth.

Milestones are a bridge that spans our past and future selves. We stand on this bridge, hair streaming, chin tilted into the wind, grateful for our present—our now—while dreaming of all that's to come.

BY JULIA VANTINE

TWENTY-NINE

Hugs

y father was a rough man, left fatherless at the age of 12, and pretty much on his own thereafter.

Because of that, he was never the sentimental type. He didn't have time or the inclination to offer a pat on the back or an affectionate hug. At 6 feet and 275 pounds, he was built for work, and work he did—7 days a week—expecting my brothers and me to do the same.

That meant that growing up, I spent much of my free time laboring with him on jobs around the house—from hand-tilling our third-of-an-acre garden, to rebuilding the family car, to painting our Victorian homestead battleship gray (he got a good price on some military paint; we used it for years).

To him, working alongside someone was the best way to show you cared. The way you felt about a person was clear from the fact you spent time with the person; you didn't need to express your sentiments. As far as I know, he never did.

Except once.

I was 22, graduated from college, and leaving home for the last time. He and I had loaded my things into a U-Haul and were standing in the garage talking. Without warning, he wrapped me in his huge arms and hugged me tight. "You were always my favorite," he said. "I love you, and I'm going to miss you."

With that, he shooed me into my car then left for the house, tears in his eyes.

I was floored by his response—proud, pleased, grateful, too. Yet some small part of me also wondered why it had taken him so long to express his love.

I can accept now that it wasn't possible for him to be

warm and affectionate—his feelings were buried too deeply under the layers of a tough life. But I've also vowed not to fall into the same trap. So, I've made hugs a key part of the "vocabulary" I offer my wife and daughters.

Thanks to my father's once-in-a-lifetime hug, I've come to realize something he never could: A hug is more than mere physical touch. It is a lightning-like connection between two people. A link that expresses love, encouragement, comfort—all the emotions that can reinforce a relationship, even turn a life around.

An incredible gift like that shouldn't be suppressed. It must be shared.

BY KEVIN IRELAND

Never again will I rush a sunrise.
I now know Nature
will yield her fruits
to me only when I am
truly ready to receive them

Sunrise

y husband and I have never been big on hiking. But when our guidebook raved about sunrise over the Himalayas, we put that on the must-do list for our trip to Nepal and headed to Sarangot, a small foothill outside the town Pokhara.

We reached Sarangot at dusk, and from our griping, you would've thought we'd climbed Everest itself. Giddy from lack of oxygen, we snuggled into bed—a straw-stuffed mattress in a family barn we'd rented for 5 cents.

The next morning at 5 A.M., we awoke to total darkness. As we bustled through town with cameras in hand, I noticed the calm, gentle way the Nepalese people greeted the morning. One man boiled a huge pot of chai, and other villagers gathered around his fire, cupping their hands around small glasses of the steaming sweet elixir. It was enchanting, but not to be deterred, we joined the stream of tourists charging up to the lookout point.

The top was crowded when we arrived, but after 10 minutes of cold fidgeting, the assembled group gave up. "The cloud cover is too heavy," one said, scowling. Then one by one they scurried down the hill to the next item on their sightseeing agendas. I was dawdling, disappointed, when I noticed a small Nepalese boy still crouched on his haunches, absently playing with a twig and shooting quick glances at the clouds. He must know something we don't, I thought. I decided to wait with him.

The boy and I didn't have to wait long. Moments later, a tiny stream of golden light burned through one dense cloud, then another. Rose-colored haze warmed the backs of the clouds, and suddenly, the morning sun peeked around the side of the mountain, miles above where I'd expected it to be.

Nothing I'd seen before prepared me for the moment the clouds withdrew with bowed heads, and the majestic Himalayas were unveiled before, around, and above me. I sat in awe, not breathing, not daring to look away, certain that God had placed me here at the backdoor of Earth to show me what Heaven really looks like.

I certainly got the message. Never again will I rush a sunrise. I now know Nature will yield her fruits to me only when I am truly ready to receive them.

BY MARISKA VAN AALST

A Child's Art

 y first summer job after college was as a children's nature guide at the local organic farm. The pay was disappointing, but I got to be outside all day, and better yet, there were the thank you letters kids sent after visiting!

When the bulging manila envelopes arrived, the other guides and I would cluster under a tree to enjoy the masterpieces. We'd read aloud delightfully awkward run-on sentences and flash around images of dancing bumblebees or flower-filled fields that the children recalled from their tours.

One day, a card arrived that featured a single figure and no words. The scene was of a girl with completely outstretched arms, rushing forward to greet a school bus. The red crayon "U" of a smile the child gave her was remarkably warm, as were the giant blue circle eyes. Even the stringy yellow crayon hair was welcoming—flipped up on either side of her head, mimicking a second smile radiating from this whimsical character.

It was a nirvana of sorts when I realized the vibrant, benevolent character in this picture was me.

These days, when I feel the most beaten down, self-loathing, or bitter, it's sometimes hard to imagine that that character still exists. But she must be there if that dear child saw her. So I try to step away from whatever problem I'm handling and let my character step forward, cheerfully greeting whoever and whatever the school bus of life brings me.

We can't always rush forward with open arms to greet what comes our way in life, but it's easier to embrace disappointments when we visualize our true characters glowing inside us somewhere, abundantly loving and lovable.

BY MARY S. KITTEL

I savored his clean, new fragrance, but I knew: Fresh or funky, sweet or tangy, this slippery creature was mine. I was his.

The Smell of a New Baby

ven before my son was born, I looked forward to the first bath. It symbolized my yearning to connect with him—to make him real after so many months of waiting.

His tiny tub was at the ready. So were the baby bath, powder, and comb and brush set (purchased a full 4 months before my due date). I could already imagine the fresh smell of my new child.

Then Wyeth finally arrived, and the nurses told me I couldn't give him a full bath for 2 weeks, until his umbilical cord fell off. And so, we got by with sponge baths that disguised but never removed his unadulterated eau de baby. I was unprepared for how seductive this musky scent could be.

As I discovered, the smell of a new infant is the smell of *life*: often indelicate, infinitely precious. And whether I was inhaling the aroma of powder or something decidedly less fragrant, Wyeth's scent spoke to me of innocence and vulnerability—qualities all too rare in an adult world.

B-Day finally came. I lowered a squalling Wyeth into his tub, applied a dab of baby bath to the top of his fragile, beloved, sour little head, and began my ablutions. Five minutes later, I swaddled him in a towel, dipped my nose to his scalp, and inhaled.

He smelled like a daisy.

I savored his clean, new fragrance, but I knew: Fresh or funky, sweet or tangy, this slippery creature was mine. I was his. At that moment, he was the beating of my heart, the air in my lungs, the reason I myself had come to be. In that first awkward water dance between my son and myself, I felt as if I, too, had just been born.

BY JULIA VANTINE

THIRTY-THREE

Romance

y first experience with love was with a man whose romantic notions dated back to when knights rescued their damsels in distress.

On the evening after our first date, I was so excited that I couldn't sleep. So I retreated to the rooftop outside of my bedroom window to appreciate the full moon and the brightness of the stars. While thinking of my new love, I was startled by the sound of crunching leaves from below. Then, all of a sudden, the end of a rope landed next to me on the roof. It was my knight in shining armor.

I tied the rope around the chimney, and he climbed up onto the roof. I was so touched, I held him close to me for what seemed to be an eternity.

We then slipped back inside and lay on a blanket in front of the window where the moonlight shone brightly. We held each other in a stare and commented on the moon shadow around our bodies. The shadow appeared to be one person, which is how I felt in that moment of pure romance.

That relationship taught me how important romance is for a couple. It was through romance that I learned to overlook a partner's idiosyncrasies and instead focus on what makes him special to me. Appreciating what's "so right" in a relationship, rather than what's going wrong, helps keep love alive even in the not-so-romantic times.

Today, with a busy career, I sometimes feel like the routines of life are taking over—that the one I love is just the man I come home to, rather than the one I share the beauty of love with. That's when I stop and think of ways to share some special time with him. Whether it be through a candlelit bath or a walk in the woods, it always sets the butterflies of romance fluttering.

BY ELIZABETH B. PRICE

Whether it be through a
candlelit bath or a
walk in the woods, it always sets
the butterflies of
romance fluttering.

Holidays are more than **meals;** they are the **celebration** of togetherness.

THIRTY-FOUR

Holidays

y parents divorced when I was 5, and with my father out of the picture, my mother was my sole caregiver. She knew it was very important for me to be part of an extended family, but that wasn't the easiest thing to arrange. My father's family lived outside the Canadian province where we were, and most of my mother's family lived overseas. There were, however, two relatives in town: my widowed great-aunt and her daughter.

Over time, the four of us grew extremely close. Aunt Agnes became more like my grandmother, and she took great pleasure in making my holidays special. My mother, so talented at other things, is not renowned for her cooking. So the family Thanksgiving and Christmas meals (and more) were my Aunt Agnes's domain.

On every occasion, there would be huge quantities of my favorites. We'd have turkey, cranberry sauce, pumpkin pie—an endless appetizing list. Of course, there was always an equally huge doggie bag for us to take home at each meal's end.

As my aunt aged, I suspect that she would have stopped the holiday meals if not for me. But it was clear from the look in her eyes every time she watched me dig in that feeding me was a true pleasure for her. It was, I know, her way of making a little girl who'd known sadness feel warm and included.

In time, I was engaged and got ready to move to the United States, where my fiancé lived. I knew with all the immigration paperwork, it would be some time before I got back to Canada for another holiday meal. So the year I was to leave, I asked my husband-to-be to come to Canada to celebrate Christmas with Aunt Agnes and the rest of us.

That year, Aunt Agnes's spread was even more elaborate than usual. As we ate, we looked at each other, as if to say, "It's been wonderful, hasn't it?" We sensed a new era was beginning, and we were happy, but we didn't want this old one to stop.

I still think back on those terrific holiday gatherings with pleasure, and now I realize that holidays are more than meals; they are the celebration of togetherness. I thank Aunt Agnes for bringing my family even closer together through her meals and for helping a shy girl become a confident woman.

BY JENNIFER GOLDSMITH

THIRTY-FIVE

Trust

Every autumn, when the smell of wool sweaters and harvests are in the air, I head to the other end of the county—to take a "short cut" by the cider maker. After passing small horse farms, white stucco farmhouses, and abandoned mills that all start to look alike, the silver glimmer of his roadside refrigerator strikes familiar.

The ritual goes like this: You pull your truck alongside a barn-turned-garage, where a makeshift overhang defines the "cider shack." As if you're an old friend making an agreed-upon exchange, you help yourself to a gallon of sweet brown mirth in the fridge; the cider man counts on you to make your own change from an unlocked money box on a picnic bench.

The bench may also peddle homemade apple butter or the multicolored jewels of random canned preserves. The cider maker often offers freebies, too: turned-twig wreathes or sandwich bags of chestnuts with a "Help yourself—Merry Christmas" note.

My favorite time to fetch cider is actually after dark, when you can let the entrancing crack of light pour out from the refrigerator into the densely black, solitary countryside. The only sound is the buzz of the fluorescent light illuminating the money box, and the *ka-chink* of my coins while I satisfy a late-night thirst straight from the jug. Indulging in the freedom to swallow the unusually wild and sweet-tart bouquet of unpasteurized juice is a sacrament for even the least religious.

It seems inevitable that mischievous teenagers have pillaged the cider man's money box, or that someone dizzy with cider-lust occasionally has grabbed an extra gallon. But whatever the losses, the cider man holds to his custom of assuming his neighbors are basically good and honorable—even the ones he's never met.

You see, rural culture survives on understood reliances. It's assumed that you'll swap tools, "learn up" each other's kids, and guide a neighbor's roadside horse back to its pasture if it escapes. Cityfolk and countryfolk alike all depend on human bonds like these. After all, nourishing our need for security and our need for beauty, our deepest material and spiritual thirsts take constant exchanges. When we withhold trust out of fear or cynicism, our humanity starves.

If, like the cider man, we continue to set out our best handiwork for one another and hope for the best, there will always be enough cracks of light left in the dark to lure good neighbors to one another's harvests.

BY MARY S. KITTEL

Sympathy

Years ago, my wife and I owned a flower shop. Shortly after opening the doors for the first time, I came to love many things about our business: being surrounded by breathing colors; the pleasure of helping people celebrate their most joyful moments; the contented tiredness that crashed ashore after the Valentine's Day madness was over. But there was one thing I dreaded.

Funerals.

What could I say to people who were suffering the most unspeakable of losses? What could I do when the words they needed to say were lost in heartbreaking sobs?

How should I respond when I, a complete stranger, had no way of truly knowing what they were going through?

To say that I felt awkward and useless is a giant understatement. I had no idea how to express appropriate sympathy, or even if I should. Then about a year after we opened, we hired a most remarkable woman who showed me the right way to react.

Wendy was good with people. She had an easy smile, a delightful sense of humor, and an immediate camaraderie with each person who walked into our store, no matter their walk of life.

She talked and talked and talked as she helped customers, and when they left, they were almost always smiling. I know; I watched. There was only one time I heard her fall silent: the first funeral flower order she took.

The family came in to select the arrangements they wanted. The woman whose husband had died was struggling dearly to keep her voice intact long enough to place the order. It wasn't long before she broke down.

Wendy didn't say a word. She moved from behind the

counter to find a chair for the woman. She eased her into it. She sat beside her and let her cry. Quiet, not speaking. She brought tissues when they became necessary. She touched the back of her hair when the moment asked for it.

The woman's crying slowly came to a stop. She wiped her eyes, and she looked at Wendy. And she smiled. Just a little one. And she said, "Thank you."

It was then that I realized that sympathy doesn't mean *saying* anything. There isn't anything you *can* say to help someone through grief, whether it be a death, a divorce, or a lost job. Sympathy asks for only one thing—your presence. To find a chair when necessary. To supply a tissue, a home-cooked meal, a walk in the park. To offer a caring hand and a warm embrace.

You don't need to worry about having the right words. Just bring yourself.

BY CHRISTIAN MILLMAN

Holding hands is usually considered a romantic gesture. But in the right situation, it can mean so much more.

THIRTY-SEVEN

Holding Hands

A ndrea and I have been best friends for as long as I can remember. Ever since our fathers worked together at an Air Force base in California, we have had a unique bond, always knowing the thoughts on one another's minds. As roommates, however, our friendship was put to the ultimate test.

I wasn't fond of her messy habits, and I let her know it. She didn't like my boyfriend, and she let me know it. For a while, we couldn't even talk to each other without a fight erupting.

All that fell to the wayside one morning when I got a

call from home and learned that our lifelong friend, Tim, had been killed in a car accident.

As the tears began to well up in my eyes, Andrea clasped my hand tightly in hers, and she wouldn't let it go. With her hand wrapped around mine, we both cried, releasing all our sorrow over the loss of a good friend. Holding my hand was more powerful than any words she could have said to me.

Holding hands is usually considered a romantic gesture. But in the right situation, it can mean so much more. In this case, it eased my sorrow and restored a friendship that has been strong ever since.

BY KELLEY CALLOWAY

T H I R T Y - E I G H T

Charity

hen I was in my early thirties, I spent several months working with an outreach team treating the homeless mentally ill in New York City. Our team consisted of two nurses, Terri and Anne Marie, and a psychiatrist, a kindly M.D. from Haiti whom everybody called Dr. Paul. I was the driver and recruiter.

Each night, we would arrive at a different homeless shelter and set up a portable clinic. I would circulate among the ragged, struggling, lonely men and women who were staying there, telling them that free physical exams were available as well as treatment for cuts, colds, and other minor health problems. The real goal, however, was to convince anyone who was clearly delusional to sit down for a chat with Dr. Paul. He, in turn, would try to get them to accept medication or hospitalization.

What always amazed me about this job was how good it made me feel. I can't remember ever leaving a shelter not feeling exhilarated.

That experience taught me an important lesson about charity: It is an act of compassion that intrinsically is linked to action. To simply sit down and write a check for some organization is a good thing, no question. Genuine charity, though, occurs when we *actively* manifest God's love in the world. We know this is God's work because it turns the laws of the physical universe upside down. Instead of feeling drained by the energy we expend in an act of charity, we are filled.

That's why I can honestly say that the homeless people I met in those New York shelters did far more for me than I ever did for them.

BY DOUG HILL

We know this is God's
work because it turns the laws of
the physical universe upside down.
Instead of feeling drained
by the energy we expend in
an act of charity,
we are filled.

THIRTY-NINE

Summer Nights

ur back yard went on forever—a long grassy plot just across the alley from the O'Connor girls. My sister and I spent our summers searching for four-leaf clovers by daylight and wishing on the first stars of night. Our backyard was a refuge from a house that wasn't always filled with happiness.

We relished those late, starlit nights when it was too hot and muggy to go inside. Our mother would call us in, but we'd beg to stay out a little while longer. We were searching, we'd explain. For what? We couldn't say; we just sensed that the warm summer nights of childhood were meant to be enjoyed. Well, if you're going to stay outside, then look for shooting stars, our mother suggested.

We'd peer deep into the dark, clear, summer sky, look-ing among the blaze of twinkles for that special flaming trail of a star burning above us. In all those summer nights, I never saw a shooting star. But it didn't matter because each time I fell asleep in the cool grass, convinced that wishes were made to come true.

BY ELLEN MAZO

There were lessons in so much of what my dog did, but the key one surely was the importance of living in the moment of extracting all the joy possible from each experience.

FORTY

Old Dogs

When my old golden retriever developed major health problems, I knew that watching him fail would be painful, but I wasn't prepared for the powerful lessons he'd offer in the last year of his life.

Chance was 14 when the problems started. First, he developed a thyroid tumor that collapsed his throat and left him whistling for breath. Then came cataracts in both eyes, arthritis in his hips, and a series of ministrokes that threw off his balance. Any one of these setbacks would have left me pleading for relief, but Chance became more serene as the disabilities piled up—seemingly seizing each problem as an opportunity to demonstrate how to face aging with dignity and grace.

When hip pain left him frozen on the floor, unable to rise for a quick pet as I came home, he didn't complain. He just lay there patiently, beckoning me with his thumping tail, each stroke spelling out the value of waiting for the things you want.

When his cataracts made navigating difficult after dark, he'd stand calmly until I could guide him inside, proving how easy it is to find contentment if you let go of your pride and insecurities and learn to lean on those who love you.

When ministrokes had him staggering like a drunk, he taught the value of persistence. For days after each attack, he'd lurch and fall as he moved about. Yet again and again he'd try to walk, each day moving a few more steps until finally he was able to get outside and back by himself.

There were lessons in so much of what he did, but the key one surely was the importance of living in the moment—of extracting all the joy possible from each experience—whether it's a day lazing under a warm sun or a few minutes savoring a favorite meal.

For most of our life together, Chance was always rushing ahead, searching out new adventures, then circling back to let me know what lay around the next bend. As an old dog, he did the same thing, using his attitude, instead of his once-fast legs, to show the way. For this, I'll be forever grateful.

BY KEVIN IRELAND

The tastes, **the aromas,** the setting, and the calm of these times are **soothing breaks** from the usual rushed meals I eat when I'm on my own.

FORTY-ONE

Family Dinners

hen I was growing up, my parents always insisted that our family eat dinner together as often as we could. Those times were filled with the ethnic dishes of my ancestors, providing tangible proof of who I am. I no longer live at home, but when I visit, family dinners are just as meaningful. And we still carry on the tradition of preparing the meal the way my parents began doing it so many years ago.

We always start the day at the farmer's market. Sometimes we pick up pasta and tomatoes to make recipes that came from my mother's Italian relatives, and other times we buy sauerkraut and Polish sausage for dishes passed down from my father's Polish parents.

Then we head home to fill the house with the smell of homemade red sauce or pierogies frying on the stove. I ceremoniously set the table with Nana's red glass plates— the set she got for her 25th wedding anniversary. Then when the feast is ready, we all sit down to eat and talk and take our time enjoying each other's company.

The tastes, the aromas, the setting, and the calm of these times are soothing breaks from the usual rushed meals I eat when I'm on my own. Just as important, my family dinners provide the time to connect to the people I love and to feel my ancestral roots.

BY MARIE SUSZYNSKI

FORTY-TWO

A Good Cup of Coffee

hroughout my teenage years, my mother always had a steaming pot of coffee ready when I got home from school.

My mother, brothers, sisters, and I would sit around the big dining room table and drink and talk for hours. It was our bonding session. We shared stories about every aspect of our lives. My mother lectured us on some of the friends we kept, and we told her to loosen up. Somehow, we could talk about anything over a cup of coffee and leave the table without holding grudges.

Our coffee talks became a tradition, and as I got older, my conversations with Mom matured. I went from talking

Somehow, we could talk about anything over a cup of coffee and leave the table without holding grudges.

about my boyfriend to discussing my husband. The connection between us became deeper and deeper with each cup we shared.

I guess all of us have something that reminds us of our mothers—whether it's the smell of her perfume or the charm she wore around her neck. For me, it's coffee. The smell gives me a warm and cozy feeling and helps me remember all my special conversations with Mom. Just as important, it reminds me of the power that a good cup of coffee has when you share it with someone you love.

BY NANCY GREEN

Curiosity is
a gift we each can share.
Harvesting it is simple:
Just be like a child.
Wonder, play,
pretend,
and live in the moment.

FORTY-THREE

Curiosity

hen I was growing up, I would pretend I was from another planet, reporting all about life here on Earth. I found my curiosity sparked by the most mundane of things: the weird pops and thuds of refrigerators, a candle's dancing flame, the perfect symmetry of a pinecone, or the giggly thrill of a trampoline.

These days, I still like to put my curiosity to use. It lets me experience and appreciate my surroundings on a deeper level. And whenever I find myself worried or stuck on a problem, it's very freeing to approach it with a curious mind.

If I'm puzzling over a situation at work, I may try to

imagine what someone I admire—like Sojourner Truth or St. Francis of Assisi—would do. Or maybe I'll consider how my dog would handle it: Be loyal to the people involved, tear the problem open, and see what's inside, maybe bury it for a little while and come back to it later.

Curiosity also helps relieve stress. If I'm anxious from thinking too much, I may relax, pretend I'm a painter for a few minutes, and just view my surroundings from that perspective. Suddenly, the world will reveal itself in a dazzling array of shapes and colors. Even the desk on which I am working will draw my interest: the long plane of the wooden top, the pattern of the grain, its warm reddish brown color, the sunlight reflecting softly on it, its blocky drawers with handles like smooth skipping stones. . . . The desk leads to the elegant long legs of the chair, which leads to the floor and so on, everything endless, touching, connected in a mysterious wordless beauty.

Looking at the world like this helps me clear my mind and get a larger perspective. Then I can calmly face the task at hand with contentment and confidence that it will work out.

Curiosity is a gift we each can share. Harvesting it is simple: Just be like a child. Wonder, play, pretend, and live in the moment. Then watch with amazement as the world unfolds around you.

BY KARA MARANTHA MESSINGER

My sister and I would hear **footsteps** on the roof, the sound of jingle bells, and then a **loud knock** at the front door.

FORTY-FOUR

A Sense of Wonder

hristmas is a special time for any kid, but when I was young, it was even more magical. Each year, during the weeks leading up to Christmas, Santa Claus would make several appearances, announcing each with a "knock-knock." My sister and I would hear footsteps on the roof, the sound of jingle bells, and then a loud knock at the front door. When we'd open the door, no one would be there, but there would be a gift for each of us.

It didn't take long before my friends became inquisitive about our special treatment: "Santa Claus comes to your house *before* Christmas? How many times?

Does he bring Mrs. Claus?" The questions never ended.

So one day I asked my dad: "Why doesn't Santa Claus go to my friends' houses, too?"

"I don't know—maybe we should say something to him," he said. Sure enough, soon after he and I wrote to Santa, Santa was knock-knocking on all my friends' doors, too. We were completely taken with the wonder of it all.

I guess I never noticed that my dad was out a little more often during the evenings before Christmas. I also didn't think anything was awry when one night he came home wet and dirty—how would I have guessed he had fallen in a neighbor's septic tank during a knock-knock getaway? I truly believed it was Santa.

My dad's knock-knocks added extra excitement to the already electric Christmas season. They also filled me with a sense of wonder I still love to recall. When I have children, I suspect Santa will do knock-knocks at my house, too. I just hope I can climb up on the roof as effortlessly as Dad did.

BY ELIZABETH SHIMER

Hope

othing in my life had prepared me for what I had to do. Choosing my words carefully, and fighting to maintain my composure, I told my 4-year-old daughter that her grandmother had suffered a stroke, that she was in a coma, and that the doctors said she would probably never wake up. As she snuggled into her bed, Amelia looked at me, eyes bright, and said, "Maybe Grandma will be okay."

"Maybe she will," I said, choking back the tears. But I knew better. I was flying up to Myrtle Beach, South Carolina, from our Florida home in the morning to say good-bye to my mom.

The rest of that awful week, I joined my brother and father sitting by my mother's side in the hospital room. I held her hand and talked to her. I told her that we still needed her. I told her that it wasn't time to leave yet. I told her how much I loved her. And I told her that her little granddaughter, Amelia, believed that she'd get better.

The doctors, with all their years of training and experience, offered no hope for recovery. The damage was simply too extensive.

Then, a couple of weeks later, an odd thing happened. Mom woke up. She came out of the coma, persevered through a long and arduous rehabilitation, during which she had to learn to walk, read, and write all over again, and eventually returned home to Dad.

The only one who wasn't shocked was Amelia. The doctors couldn't explain it. Amelia didn't need to. Hope came as naturally to her as breathing.

So why are we so afraid to hope sometimes? Maybe it's because over the years, life's disappointments can turn us to disillusionment. How many times have you heard someone say: "Hope for the best, expect the worst"? That's not really hope at all.

Hope is being able to look at our world with all of the joy and wonder of a child.

BY JACK CROFT

Relations don't end;
they just take
different, more
intimate forms.

FORTY-SIX

Companionship

y father had traveled to many exotic places, photographing African hippos and sifting through ancient stones at the Coliseum in Rome, but he had never seen my office. Three years ago, I invited him to my job. Before he could visit, though, he died.

His death was sudden and stunningly painful: I felt robbed of a last chance to thank him for his protective cloak of wisdom and love. After the funeral, my days were filled with brittle attempts to push myself through the motions of day-to-day life. Then, on my first day back to work, I began to find solace.

Pulling the building door open, I spoke to him in my heart: "Here we are Dad. This is the reception area I walk through every morning." Then I pointed out paintings and hallways as I escorted him up the stairs to see my office for the first time. And so, I started a profound companionship with him that has sustained me ever since.

Dad now meets friends he had never known, witnesses frustrations I had never spoken to him about, and sees my daughter's small triumphs that he might have missed in life. His travels as my daily companion have been the most precious and wondrous trips we've ever shared.

Trying to regain momentum in your life after a great loss is about as easy as ignoring a snakebite. But if you recognize that your loved ones remain with you always—that the ties you hold with them defy the mortal weight of fear and judgment that burden others—you'll find the relations don't end; they just take different, more intimate forms.

BY SANDRA SALERA LLOYD

F O R T Y - S E V E N

Home

 friend of mine has a funny way of talking about landscape design. He tells people to picture the outdoor setting in which they feel most at home. Many picture woods and water, while others think of the beach, the mountains, or the desert blazing with color at sunset. Some think of the tranquil grasslands of the prairies, rippling like water with every breeze.

Once they have sketched their special places—the outdoor settings that capture their inner selves—my friend asks them to take their visions home to their own backyards. If you dream of a rocky coastline, he'll suggest

Many people think of home
as a **place to stay...**
It is more than that.
Home is a **place to _be_.**
A place where we can
most truly be ourselves.

adding a pebble-strewn "shore" and a water garden with a fountain to bring the sound and movement of water to life. If a serene woodland setting brings you home, he'll recommend a grove of trees and woodland undergrowth—ferns, shade-loving wildflowers, shrubs to shelter birds, perhaps some moss-strewn rocks—with a path to lead you, seemingly ever deeper, to an open glade where the sun can fill the space with light.

Many people think of home as a place to stay. But as my friend reminds us, it is more than that. Home is a place to *be*. A place where we can most truly be ourselves.

BY ELLEN PHILLIPS

Then there were
monarchs, the majestic
queens of the field.
They effortlessly glided from
flower to flower,
always inspiring
with their beauty.

FORTY-EIGHT

Butterflies

When I was a scraped-knee, blond-pig-tailed kid, there was an open plot at the end of my block that was left to flower. It was a small field in comparison to a meadow, but within a small city—where it wasn't meant to be—it seemed huge.

All kinds of wildflowers prospered there, from ivory Queen Anne's lace and purple clover, to yellow buttercups and black-eyed Susans, to burnt orange Indian paintbrushes and those light-blue flowers that seem to be so rare these days. To this field came dozens of butterflies. There were the regular white ones and pale yellow ones—all of these were easy to catch with our hands and seemed to flutter aimlessly, not even caring if they landed on a nectar-bearing flower. Then there were monarchs, the majestic queens of the field. They effortlessly glided from flower to flower, coyly evading our nets—always inspiring with their beauty but never close enough to touch.

One summer day, there must have been a mass hatching or a migration because the air was filled with orange and black waves as the monarchs sailed through the neighborhood. They were everywhere—in the trees, on the bushes nearby, even dancing in the air right in front of me. It was like a dream.

Now, when things around me seem gray, I remind myself of that day. I look through my child's eyes back to the magic of the monarchs and know that beauty truly exists.

BY JENNIFER S. KUSHNIER

FORTY-NINE

Courage

isitors to my Pennsylvania community have come to regard the 95 horse-and-buggy-driving Mennonite families here as "quaint." I'll admit, it is sweet to pass barefoot children playing beside an authentic country schoolhouse, and it's charming to buy bread that has been baked by a gentlewoman in a long dress.

But after getting to know the Mennonites, I'm more overcome by the fact that these "plain people" are the most resolute radicals among us.

Their faith teaches them to live *in* the world but not be *of* it. That so often means turning down the convenience, comfort, and glamour of the latest advancements and saying, "Our simple traditions are good enough."

While the world insists that change is not only fashionable but required for survival, "plain folks" have the guts to put their lives on the line by trusting that their ways will sustain them. And why shouldn't they? A modern world of computers, cell phones, and SUVs may be swirling around them, but nothing has come along that has proven superior to their foundations of honesty, faith, hard work, and commitment.

It's not that my neighbors are against change itself. After all, they'll purchase a stronger tractor when appropriate and even relocate to other communities. But before they make a big decision, they usually bring it to their elders, who consider how that change will affect the community as a whole.

The world rewards risk takers. But doesn't true courage require the element of wisdom? My neighbors have the wisdom-based courage to dig their heels in the soil while the outside world whizzes past. They're content with the choice they've made and are willing to deliver a quietly courageous message to the rest of us: God bless you if you go ahead. But I need to stay put because the others are counting on me here.

BY MARY S. KITTEL

Happiness is a choice, and you are the one who's responsible for it.

FIFTY

You

top 'shoulding' on yourself!" my friend yells whenever she catches a whiff of someone doing something just because they think they should.

I know what she's saying. I used to "should" on myself quite a bit.

Rather than focusing on my needs or my dreams, I put my energy into doing what I thought I should do: what was "right" to make my relationships work, please my family, win acceptance from my peers, get into the right college, and get the job that provided the most security.

Because my heart wasn't in my choices, life situations

seldom worked out. I was miserable in school then chronically late when I started work. My relationship with my boyfriend failed, and I became more and more unsure of who really were my friends. I finally hit bottom when I became ill with chronic fatigue syndrome. Exhausted, lonely, and depressed, I staggered around in a stupor for weeks.

Then one day at my parents' house, I noticed a small blue book that had fallen from the shelf: *Heal Your Body* by Louise Hay.

It changed me forever.

Hay explains the importance of accepting and loving yourself—of making decisions because *you* want to do something, regardless of what others might think. She recommends that you say, "I love and approve of myself." Everyday. Hundreds of times.

How silly her suggestion seemed. But at that point, I was willing to try anything. So each time I started thinking about how others might view what I was doing, I would stop and say, "I love and approve of myself."

Amazingly, by the end of the first day, I felt better than I had in years, emotionally and physically. Soon I became stronger and more grounded than I ever had been. I had energy, I was buoyant with hope, and I lit up with this firecracker of truth that I'll share with you: Happiness is a choice, and you are the one who's responsible for it—not some boyfriend, spouse, family, or friends. You!

As long as you keep in mind the importance and value of you, you will handle anything that the world throws your way. You will succeed because of the power, the spirit, and the vision of *you*.

BY KARA MARANTHA MESSINGER

· Saying "I'm Sorry" · Flowers · Motherhood · A Good Book · Kindness

· Afternoon Naps · Family · Thunderstorms · Sad Movies · Friends · Gratitude · Quiet Time

· Independence · Imagination · Contentment · Milestones · Hugs · Sunrise

· A Child's Art · The Smell of a New Baby · Romance · Holidays · Trust · Holding Hands

· Charity · A Good Cup of Coffee · Summer Nights · Old Dogs · Family Dinners

· Curiosity · A Sense of Wonder · Hope · Companionship · Home · Butterflies · Courage

· You · Wisdom · Warm Spring Days · Memories · Honest Work · Charity · Faith

· Bubble Baths · Passion · Puppies · Seashells · Candlelight · Saying "I Love You" · Wisdom

· Butterflies · Flowers · Motherhood · A Good Book · Kindness · Afternoon Naps

· Holidays · Thunderstorms · Sad Movies · Family · Gratitude · Quiet Time · Independence

· Imagination · Contentment · Milestones · Hugs · Sunrise · A Child's Art

· The Smell of a New Baby · Romance · Holidays · Trust · Sympathy · Flowers · Charity

· Summer Nights · Old Dogs · Family Dinners · A Good Cup of Coffee

· Curiosity · Home · Butterflies · Courage · You · Wisdom · Warm Spring Days · Memories

· Honest Work · Faith · Bubble Baths · Passion · Puppies · Seashells · Candlelight

· Charity · Flowers · Motherhood · A Good Book · Kindness · Afternoon Naps · Wisdom

· Friends · Thunderstorms · You · Warm Spring Days · Gratitude · Quiet Time

· Independence · Imagination · Contentment · Milestones · Hugs · Sunrise · A Child's Art

· Wisdom · The Smell of a New Baby · A Good Book · Holidays · Trust · Sympathy